You're Not Dead Yet

Heaven Is the Finish Line:
The Homerun of Your Dreams

Spiritscribe Publishing, LLC
P.O. Box 2241
Humble, Texas 77347
www.spiritscribepublishing.com
(832) 445-6229

ISBN 978-0-692-87452-3

Larson Family

You're Not Dead Yet

Heaven Is the Finish Line:
The Homerun of Your Dreams

Millie Smith Larson

Acknowledgments

I acknowledge my One and only Jesus Christ: He is the one who gave me life, hope, healing, and deliverance. I also acknowledge my seven (7) lovely daughters, my super friend Fernandez King, all of my grandchildren, and great grandchildren. I cannot forget my pastor Dr. Lester Roch and Sharon Roch for26 years.

Introduction

This book is written to encourage you to know it is never too late to take charge of your life and become what you were meant to be: A child of the King, Jesus Christ. If you picked this book or someone gave it to you (regardless of how you received it), you're not dead yet! If someone reads it to you, hands it to you, or you read it yourself, it will change your way of thinking: spiritually, you are dead to sin (Leviticus 15:3) if you accepted Jesus into your life. You can live a variety of different ways, but you are not really living until you become a friend of God and get a personal relationship with him. You are still alive and can still hear voices until you take your last breath.

Change Your Battery. Make Your Sparks Fly. (Acts 2:2)

Psalms 149 through 150 tells us how to praise God. We should worship him in spirit and truth during the good times and the bad times. Praise and worship in all things. You can praise your way out of anything. One person has a reason for something not being done. Another person has a reason for being unable as well, but it can be done with God's help. "My help cometh from the Lord" (Psalms 121). Get up and do something for Jesus. This is your life: Do not trust it with just anyone.

Some people need a short-range project. Some want a long-term project, so they can see the progress. You need to meet needs, quickly. Jesus is a long-term (life-long) project. Try Jesus before you try the rest; he is the best. Do not say "Well, I'll get around to it." Do not miss out on this moment. Jump in, now. You only have today. Tomorrow may be too late. Jesus is waiting on you.

He is there all of the time. His line is never busy, and he does not have an answering machine. You call; he answers. It is just that simple. One of my nephews was just coming to church and sitting in his seat at all times, so I went over asked him what he was waiting on. He replied "Jesus." I told him "No, Jesus is waiting on you." He got up, went to the altar, and gave his life to Jesus.

Later, he became a preacher in 1978. He has been with Jesus ever since then. He has been having his own church for a long time, now. I have never seen a man as humble as him. You may say, "Oh, I feel so bad; I never dreamt this would happen to me." Keep breathing and look around yourself. You might lose your breath when you see what some people are going through.

Jesus has blessed me to write around fifteen songs. One of them is "How Can I Stop Loving God?" Be a servant, now! Do not refuse it. Someone wants to serve you. Everyone should be a servant. "Train up a child in the way he should go and when he is old he will not depart from it" (Proverbs 22:6).

I am free; no more chains are binding me (John 16-29). You are free from bondage and sin. Jesus died to set us free. "No weapon that is formed against thee shall prosper..." (Isaiah 54:17). Everyone needs someone, and you can be that someone. Trust me. I have been through unimaginable things, but someone needed me at that time.

Be open minded. Someone loves you besides Jesus. Show your love to someone. Everybody needs a hug, a compliment, or a pat on the back. That makes them feel like doing more good things. Learn to accept compliments; for instance, you can say "Thanks, I feel great!" if someone says "You look great, today."

If someone says "You sure have lost weight" to you, you can reply by saying "Thanks, I have been working on it." That is if you have been. Short Circuit: Do not rush through your work just to say you have done it. You should do it well regardless of how long it takes. Take pride in whatever you do, even if it is flipping a burger or cutting the grass because honesty is the best policy in every instance. No one may ever know you or see your works, but God does.

Work On These Ten Things to Win People to Christ.

1. Keep sin out of your own life. Do not let your good be spoken of, wickedly.

2. Love people regardless of their condition.

3. Serve people. Someday, you might be on the other end.

4. Encourage others often. This really makes someone want to do more and do it better.

5. Pray for friends and enemies (Matthew 5: 44-45).

6. Make someone laugh. It is good for the soul and the body (Proverb 17:22).

7. Build up one another: "You did a great job!" "How did you do that?"

8. Spread the Word of God (Isaiah 11:9). Do not place yourself in the position to hear God say you did not even try to get the word out.

9. Be fruitful. (Women) Push like you are in labor. You can do it!

10. Children grasp things at ten more than any other age. Plant your seed and do not dig it up (Mark 4:16). Tell the Devil "if you do not believe my seed will grow, just sit back and watch (Genesis 11:31).

Do not let your child feel like no one appreciates them. He or she will go out and find someone who will. Therefore, they will cling to the wrong person. Be observant.

(Stay on top of things) You cannot do that by abusing your body. Honor God with your body. Your body was purchased by God, and He owns it. Dedicate it to Him. Take care of your physical body. Maintain your body's ideal weight. Have the self discipline to eat to live, not live to eat. You would not put lead gas in your car, would you? (1 Corinthians 15:53) Eat healthy and you'll be healthy. (Turn your tests into testimonies).

(Miracles and Testimonies) The evidence of a miracle (Hebrews 11:1) says "Now, faith is the substance of things hoped for, the evidence of things unseen." "All things are possible with God" (Luke 18: 27).

Do not Miss This Moment! Jump In!

God has never made the wrong decision, but we do. We have to trust God to take us in the right direction. If things do not work out, remember God is in control of your life. Sometimes, He says *yes.* Sometimes, he says *no.* Sometimes, he makes us wait, but He knows what is best for us. You cannot really love until you get born again and begin to love yourself. If your prayers are not being answered, check your love life. Do you love Jesus, your friends, and your enemies?

Tithe First

"Give and it shall be given unto you..." (Luke 6:38). This does not mean you should give to everybody and everything. Support your church where you are a member. Give to the mission so that they can hear the Word of God. Take care of your family before anyone or anything else. Let God lead you in what to give. God does not accept things that are grudgingly given: It is better for you keep it for yourself.

First, kill the weed. Then, sow the seed because the weed will overtake the seed. Kill the curse to receive the blessing (Deuteronomy 11: 26-28). Let's live by the Word, dwell by the Word, and dig into the Word. We are saved by the Word of God.

The Banners: Praise God with them (Psalms 20:5). Do not let others rent space in your heart. Be relieved of negativity. Let us live the way we want to die. (Jeremiah 24:7) Everyone wants something in return when they give. God even wants something in return.

Get all you can get, and sit on the lid by yourself. Don't give up on your healing since you are still alive. Do not respond like Naaman did to God telling him what to do to get healed. Sometimes, it might sound unreasonable, but if you do it anyway, like Naaman listening to God's instructions, you will receive your healing. "Obedience is better [much better] than sacrifice" (1 Samuel 15:22).

The Holy Ghost! The Comforter (John 14)

A woman marries a man, hoping he will change. A man marries a woman hoping she will change. Look deep before you leap. The Holy Spirit will lead and guide you (Psalms 23). (1 Corinthians 3) Does inadequacy give you a feeling suggesting you are not good enough, etc?

Don't Tell God What to Do

Make yourself available watch him work. Do not underestimate your abilities. I can erase a mistake on paper, but I cannot erase my sins; however, Jesus can blot them out. When you fall, just get up and try, again. I never learned to ride a bicycle because I was afraid of falling, repeatedly. I gave up and gave in.

Never look down on anybody unless you are picking them up. Let brotherly love continue. (Thessalonians 4:9). Sometimes, I wear shoulder pads (they are not wings). I earned these angel wings. My angels lead and guide me, everyday. Sometimes, I think I'm going in the wrong direction, but I arrive in the right place.

Minister Kent Louis of Apostalic Tabernacle is a prime example someone can be wild and crazy and still get the Holy Spirit moving, get souls saved and baptized in the name of Jesus. You would think "Is he really in the Spirit?" when he is preaching. Yes, you can have fun and still be in the Spirit. "Make a joyful noise in the Lord" (Psalms 100:1). God made man. (Genesis 1:26) I am a cake baker. I do a lot of creating and enjoy it like Jesus did when he created us. Have you made the decision to serve him (Jesus, The Lord of Lords)? Do it now, please!

Tomorrow is not promised to you. (Matthew 6: 27-34)

You have a deadline to meet. (James 4:13-15) You're not dead yet! Call Jesus to make your appointment, today! His line is never busy, and he does not have an answering machine. "Since you have not run out of years yet, do not let your family have to run out of tears." Forgiveness makes you free. (Psalms 103:3) "Whatsoever a man soweth, that shall he reap" (Galatians 6:7).

Faith is acting upon what you believe. I believe my truck will start when I enter and turn the key. I grew up believing if my right hand itched, I would receive some money. Therefore, I look for it and get it, every time. So why not believe Jesus died for your sins, your forgiveness, and healing?

Women, if the king likes you, who cares who does not like you? (The Book of Ester). She went from rags to riches in one day. (She was working for the King, and he saw she was good for him).

The Number of Completion!

#7 is the number of completion. It is used ten times in the Bible. God completed the Earth in seven days. Naman dipped himself in the Jordan River seven times, and he was healed because of his obedience. God will forgive us seventy-seven times a day. There are seven days in the week. There is a song called "Seventy Plus Seven." I have seven daughters. If it is God's will, it is His bill.

Testimonial Section

I will tell you about my house, furniture, truck price, and all. We must dispose of our garbage and get rid of everything that is not like Jesus. Are you ready for your miracle? I have got mine and plenty of them.

Make a u-turn. Turn your life around before Jesus comes to town, or you will still be around and caught up in sin as it binds you up, completely. This is because you are going in the wrong direction. Do not recreate the actions of Sodom and Gomorrah (Genesis 13: 9-11). **Be a satisfied customer: shop in the store of Jesus Christ.**

Testimonies

#1

I was the age of sixteen when I became a friend of God, baptized, and filled with the Holy Ghost. My first of seven daughters was premature. I was nineteen-years-old and straight from down home: Hearne, Texas has a population of 486. Houston has been my home since 1962. The doctors said my child might not live because babies do not come in seven-and-a-half months.

That was a strange time, after being in labor for two days with severe pain and no pain medication at all. I finally had her: Regina. She had to stay in the hospital for a while. The doctor said my baby probably would not make it, but "God did it!" That is one of my favorite songs. Well, so much for that.

The father never came home, so it was just me. It was alright as long as he was in the army because they sent me a check, but I had to make it on my own when he got out. There were times I thought God had left me, but he was there the whole time "Waiting Patiently in Line" (another favorite song).

I came to Houston to live with my sister before the first child was born. I went back to Hearne, Texas to live with the father's mother, which turned out to be a nightmare. I came back to Houston, Texas. This time, I said, "God, I want my children and I to have our own place," and he provided that.

It was almost unbelievable, but he sent a man to show me a better way. This is where I met and married my next five children's father who had one, already. Everything went well from that point to the present thanks to the Almighty. I had birthed six daughters and got one free. However, I always loved them all. She is deceased, now, but we had a wonderful life, together. I was born Pentecostal, but I went back on God. I fell, but I got right back up, again.

#2

One night, five of my daughters, a sister from church and I were on our way to church. We had to cross some railroad tracks. I did not see the train because I looked back to tell the children to calm down. Then, I heard screams coming from them: "A train! A train!" I had no way of saving us. It was right there.

I started to jump out, but I decided to die with my five children. The next thing I knew: the car was off of the tracks on the side of the street with no motor running. The other lady was on the other side of the train. We could see her through the train's passing wheels and undercarriage. We waited with our hands in the air.

This was in 1979, so the technology was not nearly as good as today (August 2010). Neither the girls nor I knew how the car got off of the tracks until sometime later when Ms. Lena Cole (my friend from church) came to us after the train rumbled by very fast. After a few minutes, we could talk and realized it was an angel from God who got us off of the tracks.

The only things I could see or hear were the lights and the whistle of the train. Glory to God! We are all still in the church, thirty years later:

#3

God had inspired me to write this book because there are so many people who do not know him (Jesus), personally, but you are not dead yet! My third testimony is about me stuttering forty-four years. I was two years old when my mother first told me I was stuttering. She thought it was because I almost drowned by falling in a tub of water, but I saw other people did the same thing, later.

I believe that was really the most radical thing in my life. I was married, and I had three children in 1970. People teased me about not being able to say no to _____, so I kept getting pregnant around every two years. I did try to take my life because I was so tired of feeling handicapped. I had all of my birth daughters, and I was on my third marriage in 1992.

The last marriage was to a Caucasian (White) man who attended church with me for five years. He brought us to a church named Apostalic Tabernacle, which was located on 5547 Cavalcade Street in our city: Houston, Texas. The pastor's name is Lester Roch. This is a powerful, testimonial, tongue-talking, Holy Ghost filled church.

God let me know that was where I would remain after visiting many churches in Houston upon our arrival there. Pastor Roch prayed for me, and I no longer stuttered as a result. I did not know I was healed, initially. God began to use me in different ways in the church. I taught Sunday school, worked with the food pantry, worked with nursing home ministry, youth staff, and went door to door talking with people.

We had a gospel on wheels during one Saturday. I was singing and playing my tambourine, which I am still doing in February 2017, presently.

Somewhere, I realized my last marriage was not ordained by God during its course. My husband left Apostalic Tabernacle Church, and I chose to stay because I knew God had planted me there. We started becoming more distant to one another, and we finally divorced after he began doing ungodly things. This was fifteen years ago. Presently, I am still praising Jesus in the same church after twenty-one years. I am still singing in the choir at sixty-six years of age.

I am so glad that I am not dead yet, so I can share all of these testimonies, etc. with those of you who read this book. God also healed me of gall stones and disease in both lungs, migraine headaches, and that is not all.
I have been healed of stuttering, lung disease in both lungs, self-pitying, and being proud since I have been a member of Apostalic Tabernacle.

Thank God for directing me. You are alive! Read it! Share it! Live by it and your Holy Bible, together. If you have questions, ask your pastor or Jesus.

The Provisions

I wanted a car: That Friday, I told God I needed another car. He replied when I said today: He asked what color. I said burgundy. On Friday evening, I had the burgundy, Ford Crown Victoria.

I wanted a house, but I did not specify anything when I asked God. Will he give me one? I had to do a lot of fixing up on it. One day, my neighbor, and Mr. King told me this is not your house: my good friend Brother Reuben told me this is not your house.

Then, after two years, something drastic occurred. A man came by and said this to me: "This is not your house: I just bought it." I called the owner. He said, "No, I haven't sold your house to anyone." However, he had them put my address on the papers instead of the other house they were supposed to buy.

I went to court and stayed three more months without having to pay the $600.00 per month of the initial agreement. He had me evicted to keep $1800.00 to put down on the real house that God had for me. A realtor from the church took me to look at houses. The last one on the list was the one. We (my daughter Amanda and I) use it entertain people: This is usually the singles at church.

#4

They showed us the one. We walked in and Amanda said this is the one. Later, she told me that she saw three angels standing like soldiers in the back of the house with two in the front yard. I knew they were there because nothing ever happened during our nine-year residency.

She told me they would come and help me if I ever called them. I called them many times, and they were right there. I would see their figures without seeing their real faces. "For he shall give his angels charge over thee to keep thee in all thy ways" (Psalms 91: 10-11). They will also show up in the form of a real person.

I know because it happened to me. I was at Kroger's when a man approached me and told me what to do about my marriage. I was at Home Depot when another man told me that I prayed a lot and saw angels around me. Another man instructed to never buy sugar free when I was at Walmart. He told me the real companies make the food for Walmart and put Walmart's name upon it.

That was truly a blessing. He was the store's manager, and I did not even buy store brands before that. "Be not forgetful to entertain strangers. For thereby, some have entertained angel's unaware" (Hebrews 13:2).

Satan: The Devil

"And the Lord said, Simon, Simon, behold, Satan hath desired to have you, that he may sift you as wheat..." (Luke 22:23). The most important reason for writing this book is you accepting Jesus into your life. If you have read it this far, I am sure you are convinced there are real angels, demons, good people, and Jesus people. You cannot miss this moment. Jump in with all that you have received or will receive.

Satan and All His Demons

Satan has demons that work for him. Satan (The Devil) called a worldwide convention of demons (also called little imps).

Satan: We cannot keep Christians from going to church, reading their bibles, knowing the truth, or forming an intimate relationship with God. However, we can steal their time."

Demons: How shall we do this?!

"Resist the Devil, and He will flee from you" (James 4:7).

Thirteen tactics The Kingdom of Darkness will do to keep Christians distracted exist:

1. Keep them busy (occupy their minds)
2. Tempt them to spend and borrow
3. Encourage the wives to work long hours
4. Have the husbands working six or seven days per week

5. Keep them from spending time with the children
6. Excessively stimulate their minds
7. Keep the Televisions, VCRs, DVD players, Blu Ray players, and computers going, constantly.
8. Fill the coffee tables with newspapers and magazines
9. Invade their driving moments with billboards
10. Keep the wives too tired to love their husbands. (Then, they will look elsewhere.)
11. Give them Santa Clause instead of the real meaning of Christmas and the Easter Bunny so they will not know about the Resurrection's importance to power and death.
12. Involve them in gossip and small talk at the church.

It was quite a plan. The demons went eagerly to their assignments as they scattered in various directions and caused Christians to become busier and hurried. As a result, many have little time for God or their families. You can be the judge! What does *busy* mean? *Busy* means "Being Under Satan's Yoke." Stop dating Jesus and marry Him by receiving the Holy Spirit (Acts 2: 1 -21, 36-42).

Poems That God Gave Me

"Nothing Works without Work"

1. "Invest in The Best"

My life was a mess;
Till I invested in the best
I don't need a 401k
Because he is with me, everyday
I don't have lots of money,
And I don't need fame.
When I need Jesus,
I call on his name.
He is my Jehovah Jireh
He's right on time.
He's my Provider.
He keeps me in line.
He is my rock.
I just have to knock.
He'll let me in
Because he's within
You may have J P (Morgan),
But I have the best.
My interest is adding fast with J.C.
You may be on top with J.P., but
My stock does not drop with J.C. (Jesus Christ)
Please, invest in Jesus. He's the best.
Come when you get to Heaven.
You'll have a long time to rest.

2. "Stay Up in A Down Situation"

When I wrote this song in 1995, I was certainly in a down situation. My marriage had gone bad. I felt like I'd been had. I had to continue to raise my children (the ones still at home) in a biblical environment.

Things may look bad, but I'm so glad
I can stay up in a down situation.
I may be tired and weak and worn,
But I'll stay up because I am not torn.
Just sitting around. No where left to go.
But Jesus is good. Don't you know?
I made up my mind a long time ago.
I would not stay down? No way!
I'll stay up in a down situation.
The road may get rough,
But I'll stay tough.
On my knees, I beg you.
Please, fill my cup.
I'll keep running;
For I know you're coming!
So, I've gotta stay up,
And I will stay up.

Song: "Break Those Chains"

You've gotta break those chains in Jesus' name.
You can't be chained up and do God's will.
If you're chained up, you're probably still.
Listen, since I broke the chain, I'm not the same
Oh yes! I have a new name. Break the chains.
Let the world see that you have made a change.
You can't be chained up and be on the usher board,
Nor can you be chained up and reach the prisoners.
Break the chains. Let them fall. You're free.

Song: "God Is Not Good, He's Delicious"

Just like eating a candy bar,
I open my mouth wide,
Enjoy the sweet taste
You may see it on my face.
Yes, He's delicious. Believe me.
Taste and see He's real good to me.
Taste and see. You'll believe He's delicious.
I make many cakes and pies,
But they can't keep you alive.
They're so good they say,
But there's another way:
My delicious God

"You're Alive and Well"

If God work you up and let you stand on your feet or sit in your chair, you're well, today. "Bless them that curse you, pray for those who despitefully use you" (Luke 6:28). God! You have commanded me to pray for everyone, even my pastor, friends, and enemies. "In all thy ways, acknowledge him and he shall direct thy path" (Proverbs 3:6). "Standing on holy ground" (Exodus 3:5). The house of God, for example, is holy ground. Mentally, you put on unholy shoes. If my awareness of you were very serious, I would go barefoot, all of the time.

Faith: We all have a certain measure of faith whether we know it or not. All we need is as much as a grain of a mustard seed. A mustard seed is so small; it can barely be seen with the naked eye, and picking it up is hard. King James Version states "Now, faith is the substance of things hoped for; the evidence of things not seen" (Hebrews 11:1). When I started writing this book, I had faith that someday, I would finish it and get it into your hands (Matthew 17:20). This is an example of mustard seed faith. Again, it is like a mustard seed, which is less than all other seeds in comparison when it is sown in the earth (Mark 4:31).

So, you are too proud to go to the altar because your peers might think you are not saved? They are already talking about you behind your back. Let them talk. You want to grab onto more and more of Jesus while you are still alive.

Pride: "Pride goeth before destruction, and a haughty spirit before a fall" (Proverbs 16-18-19). Better it is to be of a humble spirit with the lowly than to divide the spoil with the proud." If you think you have it all together, you are wrong. You never will. The Bible says we have to pray in and out of season. "...Pray without ceasing" (1 Timothy 5:17). We are warriors for Christ. Put on the whole armor of God. If you think you need more, ask for more: whatever it is. "Ask and it shall be given unto you" (Matthew 7:7). My daughter is a prime example: "She'll ask you for anything." I thought she was spoiled, but she is not. She has more faith than the grain of a mustard seed. I am not there yet. It takes me a while to decide to ask. God owns all "...the cattle upon a thousand hills" (Psalms 50:10); I only need a few of them. Doubt makes the mountains which faith can move.

Do you feel betrayed? Sometimes, someone can betray you. I know because I have been betrayed. It is a weapon found in the hands of the one you love. Your enemy has not such tool for you. Only a friend can betray you. Betrayal is a violation of trust (an inside job). You become a victim of betrayal. You are bitten with a snake's kiss.

1. Who ever told you life was going to be easy or fair? Betrayal should not be a surprise when it occurs.
2. The best way to keep your balance is to keep your focus on another horizon.
3. Keep only cheerful friends (Matthew 7:25-34). The grouchy ones pull you down (Proverbs 17:22).
4. Laugh often, loudly, and lengthily until you gasp for breath. A cheerful heart is good medicine.

I ran track and won first place in the twenty-yard dash when I was in middle school. I was so overjoyed. Now, I am running for Jesus with my eyes on Heaven, spiritually. I have on my spiritual, running shoes (Hebrews 12:12). Let us run the race that is set before us with patience. Lord, knowing you and keeping my eyes on you enables me to run the race and cross the finish line (1 Corinthians 9:24). Run to receive the prize. Therefore, run so that you may obtain it. I have to reach my goal, and that is to be with Jesus. You should fix your eyes on the finish line; I'm fixing my eyes on Jesus.

I have eleven grandchildren. They are currently teenagers and young adults, and they adore their grandmother. None of them knew their grandfather because he passed away at a very young age. Two of them lived with me for two years while their parents were growing up. This was a joyful experience. I really wanted to keep them, but they needed to know their parents. They are very smart and intelligent. It was fun, but not easy. I was working everyday at that time. God gave me the strength to do the job.

I have twelve great grandchildren (geniuses). They are more affectionate toward me than the grandchildren. Maybe, when you get older, you will have more time, knowledge, and ability to deal with the great grandchildren. We connect really well. I don't see them, too often anymore, and honestly, I like seeing them less often. Then, I am overjoyed when I see them. Both sets of grandchildren adore me. Yes, I do spoil them. How can I not? Like my pastor says, "They should have come, first." I love the word *grandmother*. Yes! I did use the rod of correction on them! Proverbs 22:15 says withhold not correction from the child: for if though beatest him, he won't die. The rod will deliver his soul from Hell." However, praise them when they do well. I treat my sons-in-law with respect and love, and they do the same to me. They take care of me as much as possible. One of them said, "No mama...No daughter." God specified this principle in Ephesians 5:25: "husbands love your wives, even as Christ also loved the church." "Wives submit yourselves unto your own husbands" (Ephesians 5:22). You should know these things. You might be punching each other daily and think it is alright. Love and submit. It is that simple and saves marriages from stress and many other things.

God Loves You, Unconditionally

God know you, and just as he knows you; he loves every human being on this planet. There is nothing you can do to change that. The Bible says "the Lord is close to the brokenhearted" (Psalms 34:18). Jesus illustrated this personal love in the parable of the lost sheep: If a man has 100 sheep and one of them became lost, what do you think Jesus would do? Would he leave the ninety-nine others and go into the wilderness to search for the one that has strayed until he has found it? (Matthew 18:12-13) In the same way, there is more joy over one lost sinner who repents and returns to God than over ninety nine others who are righteous and haven't strayed away. God loves each of us as if there were only one to love. That means God still would have sent his Son (Jesus) to die on the cross for our sins. His love is unconditionally abiding, consistent, and everlasting. Romans 8:38-39 says I am convinced that nothing can separate us from God's love. Death, life, angels, demons, today's fears, nor our worries, or even powers of Hell will ever separate us from God's love. Now, tell me he is not serious. He does love us all. Now he did not say if we were good or bad, poor or ugly, etc.

#5

This was a very good deed, and I still think God is blessing me for this one. My oldest sister ha breast cancer. At that time, she was working in a residence with me. One day, she said "Look Millie! I have a lump in my chest." I examined it and told her maybe she should go get it checked. Believe it or not, it was cancer in a serious stage. She began chemotherapy. In months, the cancer had metastasized throughout her whole body. She was a warrior and prayed, constantly. In the meantime, her daughter, Baby girl, was declared unfit mother due to some circumstances causing C.P.S. (Children's Protective Services) to acquire her three children in their custody. My sister explained to me she would love to take them, but she could not. They were four, five, and six-years-old in 1998. Therefore, I was entering the senior stage, working two jobs, and performing church activities. However, I vowed to take them because adoption was the next step. I went through the process, and the state granted me custody of them, hoping the mother would become more suitable. I had them one year and three months. That was a challenge! My pastor said, "if I wore a hat; I would take it off to you." My sister died in 1999. She was sixty-two years old. I became a young woman after the trial of keeping the young one for that time. I called C.P.S. and told them my niece was better and could give her a chance because it was too much for me. God sent me some help from a man named George Thomas. The state did not help me. I thought I was on my own, but Jesus was there. He gave me the strength and ability take good care of them. The oldest one is in college. The second one is in music. I believe the third one is involved with music and modeling. Jesus, thank you for your help as usual.

Being at Peace

A peaceful mind generates power: "Be ye transformed by the renewing of your mind" (Romans 12:2). Accept this advice, and you will be happier and healthier.

1. Make a change in your thoughts
2. Renew your mind. Empty your mind
3. You will have a mind full of peace
4. At least twice a day, empty your mind of fears, hate, insecurities, regrets, and feelings of guilt. Forgive as God does. This will prevent unhappy thoughts and feelings from sneaking in, again.

Immediately fill your mind with creative and healthy thoughts. I have been happy, joyful, and peaceful since I have written this book because I am looking forward to seeing you happy as you read it. Your mind is shifted to neutral when the wrong thoughts are present. Say "if God loves me, I'm prosperous."

A Peaceful Mind- A Calm Repose (Quiet)

"If it be possible, as much as lieth in you, live peaceably with all men" (Romans 12:18). Repeat peaceful words that have profound suggestive power, and there is a healing in saying them.

A. Let nothing disturb you such as gossip, television, etc,.
B. Be frightened at nothing, but cautious.
C. Everything passes away except God.
D. God alone is sufficient. Create a daily practice of silence, no less than ten minutes of quiet time in one day. Think as little as possible
E. Refuse to think about lack.

About My Mother

She and my father were both sixteen when they were married, had thirteen children, raised twelve, worked until they were seventy-three years old, and they had forty-three grandchildren and great grandchildren. Her mind was still sharp at the age of ninety. She lived alone until she was ninety-four upon her death after my father passed in his seventies. I always say I'll live until I am one hundred, but I accept whatever God sees fit. I am seventy-three at this time: a baker, songwriter, potential comedian, grandmother, great grandmother, church mother, and lover of all. Peace unto you all.

Conclusion

My six daughters are simply beautiful. I raised them to be respectable and honest. Three of them are supervisors on their jobs. All of them are jewels. My firstborn daughter is deceased. She was also a spoiled beauty.